MUSIC
LISTOGRAPHY

MUSIC LISTOGRAPHY

YOUR LIFE IN (PLAY) LISTS

CREATED BY LISA NOLA
ILLUSTRATIONS BY MICHAEL GILLETTE

CHRONICLE BOOKS
SAN FRANCISCO

ISBN: 978-0-8118-6946-1

Manufactured in China

Design by Suzanne LaGasa
Illustrations by Michael Gillette

Chronicle Books endeavors to use environmentally responsible
paper in its gift and stationery products.

10 9 8 7

Chronicle Books LLC
680 Second Street
San Francisco, CA 94107
www.chroniclebooks.com

MUSIC CAN CAPTURE ENTIRE ERAS— SIMULTANEOUSLY SHAPING OUR INDIVIDUAL MOODS, IDENTITIES, LOVES, FASHION CHOICES, AND LOSSES ALONG THE WAY. FOR MANY OF US, MUSIC IS ONE OF THE BEST REASONS TO BE ALIVE. THIS BOOK WILL HELP CAPTURE THE SOUNDTRACK FOR YOUR LIFE AND HOPEFULLY BRING BACK A LOT OF FOND MUSICAL MEMORIES. I CREATED THIS BOOK AS A BIG THANK-YOU TO ALL MY FAVORITE MUSICIANS, SINGERS, AND SONGWRITERS. I HOPE YOU HAVE FUN FILLING IT IN . . .
LISA NOLA
WWW.LISTOGRAPHY.COM

THE VELVET UNDERGROUND

LIST YOUR TOP TWENTY FAVORITE BANDS

LIST THE TWENTY ALBUMS YOU'D BRING IF YOU WERE LEAVING PLANET EARTH ON A SPACESHIP

LIST YOUR TOP TWENTY FAVORITE SONGS

ARCADE FIRE, CENTRAL PARK SUMMER STAGE,
SURPRISE GUEST DAVID BOWIE 9/16/2005

LIST THE BEST CONCERTS & MUSIC FESTIVALS YOU'VE SEEN

LIST MUSIC FROM YOUR HIGH SCHOOL YEARS

JUDD NELSON'S TRIUMPHANT EXIT IN <u>THE BREAKFAST CLUB</u>
TO "DON'T YOU (FORGET ABOUT ME)"

LIST YOUR FAVORITE MUSIC MOMENTS IN FILM

"BOYS DON'T CRY" BY THE CURE
10TH GRADE GIRLFRIEND

LIST A SONG THAT REMINDS YOU OF EACH LOVER YOU'VE HAD

LIST BANDS YOU DO <u>NOT</u> LIKE

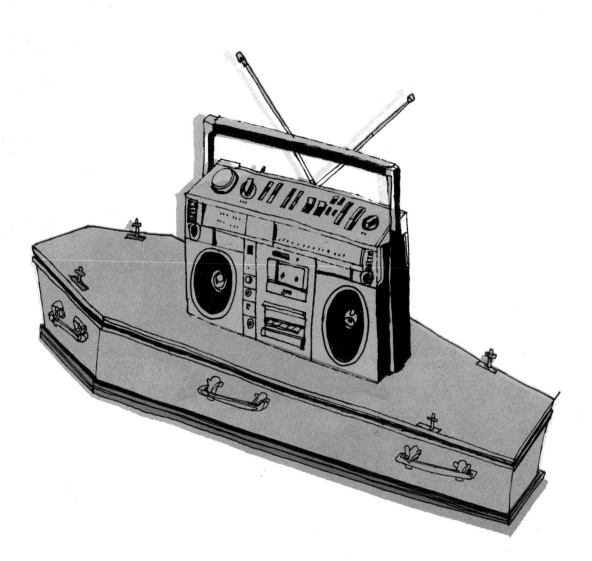

"NAKED AS WE CAME"
BY IRON AND WINE

LIST THE SONGS TO PLAY AT YOUR FUNERAL

_____

_____

_____

_____

_____

_____

_____

_____

_____

_____

_____

_____

_____

_____

_____

_____

"LOVED DESPITE OF GREAT FAULTS"
BY BLONDE REDHEAD

LIST SONGS FOR YOUR WEDDING OR COMMITMENT CEREMONY

"BY YOUR SIDE" BY SADE

LIST SONGS FOR YOUR PERFECT MAKE-OUT MIX TAPE

"LIFE'S A GAS" BY T.REX

LIST SONGS THAT COMPLETELY TRANSFORM YOUR MOOD
(A.K.A. THERAPIST IN A SONG)

I'D HELP SING SONGS OF FREEDOM
WITH BOB MARLEY & THE WAILERS

LIST WHO YOU'D LIKE TO BE A BACKUP SINGER OR DANCER FOR

LIST YOUR FAVORITE SONGS FROM THE '60S

LIST YOUR FAVORITE SONGS FROM THE '70S

LIST YOUR FAVORITE SONGS FROM THE '80s

LIST YOUR FAVORITE SONGS FROM THE '90s

BUFFALO SPRINGFIELD

LIST BANDS THAT SHOULD NOT HAVE BROKEN UP

LIST THE MUSIC YOUR PARENTS LISTENED TO WHEN YOU WERE A KID

LIST YOUR DANCE PARTY PLAYLIST

LIST YOUR COUPLES SLOW DANCE PLAYLIST

MUSIC FOR AIRPORTS BY BRIAN ENO

LIST YOUR FAVORITE INSTRUMENTAL PIECES

LIST YOUR FAVORITE SOUL & BLUES SINGERS

FREDDIE MERCURY

LIST YOUR TOP FAVORITE MALE VOCALISTS OF ALL TIME

NINA SIMONE

LIST YOUR TOP FAVORITE FEMALE VOCALISTS OF ALL TIME

FELA! THE MUSICAL

LIST YOUR FAVORITE FILM & STAGE MUSICALS

NO DIRECTION HOME : BOB DYLAN
DIRECTED BY MARTIN SCORSESE

LIST YOUR FAVORITE MUSIC BIOPICS & DOCUMENTARIES

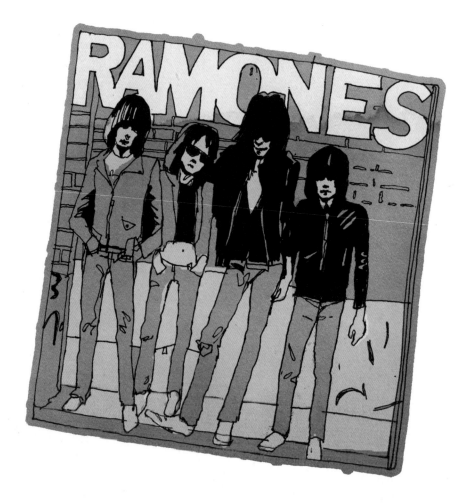

LIST THE BEST ALBUM COVERS EVER CREATED

LIST YOUR FAVORITE FASHION ICONS IN MUSIC OVER THE YEARS

LIST YOUR FAVORITE MUSIC VIDEOS

"SESAME STREET"
COMPOSED BY JOE RAPOSO

LIST YOUR FAVORITE TELEVISION & FILM THEME SONGS

"PAPER PLANES" BY M.I.A.
("BONA FIDE HUSTLER MAKING MY NAME...")

LIST SONGS YOU THOUGHT WERE ABOUT YOU (A.K.A. YOUR THEME SONG)

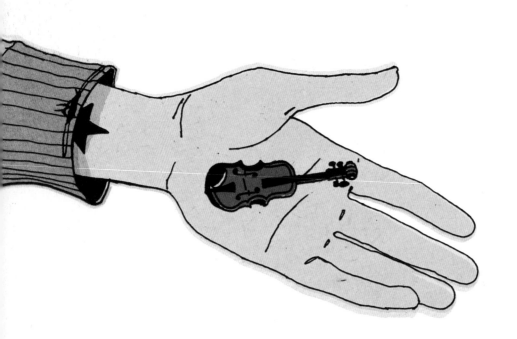

LIST THE SADDEST SONGS IN THE WORLD

"OH MY LOVE" BY JOHN LENNON

LIST LOVE SONGS YOU'D WANT TO BE SERENADED WITH

ELLIOTT SMITH

LIST PERFORMERS YOU'D BRING BACK TO LIFE

RADIOHEAD - GLASTONBURY FESTIVAL
28TH JUNE 1997

LIST CONCERTS YOU WISH YOU COULD TIME TRAVEL TO

LIST MOMENTS IN MUSIC YOU'LL NEVER FORGET

LIST YOUR KARAOKE CATALOG FAVORITES

"EYE OF THE TIGER" BY SURVIVOR

LIST YOUR MOTIVATIONAL SELF-HELP ANTHEMS!

LIST YOUR FAVORITE CONCERTS ON FILM

DOOR, DOOR BY BOYS NEXT DOOR
(LP WITH THE TRACK ""SHIVERS"")

LIST YOUR OBSCURE MUSIC DISCOVERIES

MY TICKET STUB COLLECTION

LIST THE MOST TREASURED MUSIC MEMORABILIA YOU'VE OWNED

"NUTHIN' BUT A "G" THANG"
BY DR.DRE & SNOOP DOGG

LIST THE BEST DUETS

"JOLENE" BY THE WHITE STRIPES
WRITTEN BY DOLLY PARTON

LIST YOUR FAVORITE COVER SONGS

BARBRA STREISAND

LIST YOUR GUILTY PLEASURES

LIST THE FIRST ALBUMS YOU EVER OWNED

MILES DAVIS

LIST YOUR FAVORITE JAZZ

DONNIE DARKO

LIST THE BEST SOUNDTRACKS

LIST YOUR BREAK-UP MIX TAPE SONGS

LIST ADVICE THAT YOU FOLLOW FROM LYRICS

LIST WHICH PERFORMERS YOU'D TIE THE KNOT WITH

"MY HOMETOWN" BY BRUCE SPRINGSTEEN

LIST SONGS THAT CAPTURE YOUR HOMETOWN

LIST BAND NAMES FOR YOUR FICTITIOUS BANDS

LIST THE PLACES YOU'VE SEEN LIVE MUSIC

LIST BANDS & GENRES OF MUSIC TO EXPLORE SOMEDAY

LAST
GANG
IN
TOWN

REBEL
TRUCE

THE STORY AND MYTH OF THE CLASH

MARCUS GRAY

LIST YOUR FAVORITE MUSICAL ARTIST BIOGRAPHIES

AND THIS NEXT ONE GOES OUT TO...

LIST A SONG TO DEDICATE TO EACH OF YOUR FRIENDS

LIST WHO'D PLAY AT YOUR DREAM MUSIC FESTIVAL

LIST THE SONGS THAT DRIVE YOU CRAZY

_____

_____

_____

_____

_____

_____

_____

_____

_____

_____

_____

_____

_____

_____

_____

_____

LIST YOUR FRIENDS WHO PLAY MUSIC

NOO YOIK

"FAIRY TALE OF NEW YORK"
BY THE POGUES WITH KIRSTY MACCOLL

LIST YOUR FAVORITE HOLIDAY RECORDINGS

LIST YOUR FAVORITE LIVE ALBUMS

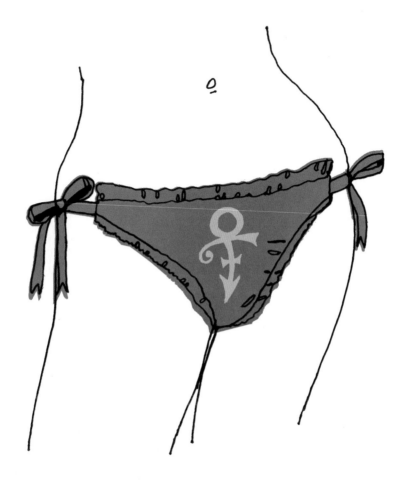

LIST SONGS YOU'D STRIP TO

PARTY PAK & NO LIMITZ

LIST THE NAMES OF YOUR DJ ALTER EGOS

LIST YOUR GUITAR HEROES

LIST PAST & PRESENT PLACES WHERE YOU FIND NEW MUSIC

SLICK RICK

LIST THE KINGS & QUEENS OF RHYMING & RAPPING

'RIKKI'

'THE VINNIE'

'THE BUBBLE'

HAIR METAL SING ALONG MIX

LIST YOUR SUMMERTIME ROAD TRIP MIX

SOFT CELL'S "TAINTED LOVE"

LIST YOUR FAVORITE ONE-HIT WONDERS

ELVIS BEFORE HE WAS DRAFTED (FORT HOOD, TEXAS)

LIST ROCK STARS YOU'VE MET